ON THE WAY TO KṚṢṆA

**HIS DIVINE GRACE
A.C. BHAKTIVEDANTA
SWAMI PRABHUPĀDA**

Founder-Ācārya
of the International Society
for Krishna Consciousness

The Bhaktivedanta Book Trust
New York · Los Angeles · London · Bombay

Library of Congress Catalog Card Number: 72-84842
International Standard Book Number: 0-912776-39-0

Readers interested in the subject matter of this book are invited by the International Society for Krishna Consciousness to correspond with its Secretary.

International Society for Krishna Consciousness
3959 Landmark Street
Culver City, California 90230

First Printing, 1973: 100,000
Printed in the United States of America
by ISKCON Press

OTHER BOOKS
by A.C. Bhaktivedanta Swami Prabhupāda

Bhagavad-gītā As It Is
Śrīmad-Bhāgavatam, Cantos 1-3 (6 Vols.)
Teachings of Lord Chaitanya
The Nectar of Devotion
Easy Journey to Other Planets
Kṛṣṇa Consciousness: The Topmost Yoga System
Kṛṣṇa, The Supreme Personality of Godhead (2 Vols.)
Transcendental Teachings of Prahlād Mahārāj
Transcendental Teachings of Caitanya Mahāprabhu
The Perfection of Yoga
Beyond Birth and Death
Rāja-vidyā: The King of Knowledge
Elevation to Kṛṣṇa Consciousness
Back to Godhead Magazine (Founder)

Complete catalogue is available upon request.

contents

1

Throughway to Happiness

Every one of us is searching after happiness, but we do not know what real happiness is. We see so much advertised about happiness, but practically speaking we see so few happy people.This is because so few people know that the platform of real happiness is beyond temporary things. It is this real happiness that is described in *Bhagavad-gītā* by Lord Kṛṣṇa to Arjuna.

Happiness is generally perceived through our senses. A stone, for instance, has no senses and cannot perceive happiness and distress. Developed consciousness can perceive happiness and distress more intensely than undeveloped consciousness. Trees have consciousness, but it is not developed. Trees may stand for a long time in all kinds of weather, but they have no way of perceiving miseries. If a human being were asked to stand like a tree for only three days or even less, he would not be able to tolerate it. The conclusion is that every living being feels happiness or distress according to the degree of development of his consciousness.

The happiness that we are experiencing in the material world is not real happiness. If one asks a tree, "Are you feeling happy?" the tree, if it could, might say, "Yes, I am happy, standing here all year. I'm enjoying the wind and snowfall very much, etc." This may be enjoyed by the tree, but for the human being it is a very low standard of enjoyment. There are different kinds and grades of living entities, and their conceptions and perceptions of happiness are also of all different types and grades. Although one animal may see that another animal is being slaughtered, he will go right on chewing grass, for he has no knowledge to understand that he may be next. He is thinking that he is happy, but at the next moment he may be slaughtered.

In this way there are different degrees of happiness. Yet of all of them, what is the highest happiness? Śrī Kṛṣṇa tells Arjuna:

sukham ātyantikaṁ yat tad
buddhi-grāhyam atīndriyam
vetti yatra na caivāyaṁ
sthitaś calati tattvataḥ

"In that joyous state *(samādhi)*, one is situated in boundless transcendental happiness and enjoys himself through transcendental senses. Established thus, one never departs from the truth." (Bg. 6.21)

Buddhi means intelligence; one has to be intelligent if he wants to enjoy. Animals do not have really developed intelligence and so cannot enjoy life as a human being can. The hands, the nose, the eyes, the other sense organs and all the bodily parts may be present on a dead man, but he cannot enjoy. Why not? The enjoying energy, the spiritual spark, has left, and therefore the body has no power. If one looks further into the matter with a little intelligence, he can understand that it was not the body that was enjoying at all but the small spiritual spark that was within. Although one may think that he is enjoying by the bodily sense organs, the real enjoyer is that spiritual spark. That spark always has the potency of enjoyment, but it is not always manifest due to being covered by the material tabernacle. Although we may not be aware of it, it is not possible for the body to experience enjoyment without the presence of this spiritual spark. If a man is offered the dead body of a beautiful woman, will he accept it? No, because the spiritual spark has moved out of the body. Not only was it enjoying within the body, but it was maintaining the body. When that spark leaves, the body simply deteriorates.

It follows that if the spirit is enjoying, it must have its senses also, otherwise how can it enjoy? The *Vedas* confirm that the spirit soul, although atomic in size, is the actual enjoying agent. It is not possible to measure the soul, but that is not to say that it is without measurement. An object may seem to us to be no bigger than a point and may seem to have no length or width, but when we perceive it under a microscope we can see that it has both length and width. Similarly, the soul also has its dimensions, but we cannot perceive them. When we buy a suit or dress, it is made to fit the body. The spiritual spark must have form, otherwise how is it the material body has grown to accomodate it? The conclusion is that the spiritual spark is not impersonal. It is an actual person. God is an actual person, and the spiritual spark, being a fragmental part of Him, is also a person. If the father has personality and individuality, the son also has them; and if the son has them, we can conclude that the father has them.

So how can we, as sons of God, assert our personality and individuality and at the same time deny them to our Father, the Supreme Lord?

Atīndriyam means that we have to transcend these material senses before we can appreciate real happiness. *Ramante yogino 'nante satyānanda-cid-ātmani:* the *yogīs* who are aspiring after spiritual life are also tasting enjoyment by focusing on the Supersoul within. If there is no pleasure, if there is no enjoyment, then what is the point of going to so much trouble to control the senses? What kind of pleasure are the *yogīs* relishing if they are taking so much trouble? That pleasure is *ananta*—endless. How is this? The spirit soul is eternal, and the Supreme Lord is eternal; therefore reciprocation of their loving exchanges is eternal. One who is actually intelligent will refrain from the flickering sensual enjoyment of this material body and fix his enjoyment in spiritual life. His participation in spiritual life with the Supreme Lord is called *rāsa-līlā.*

We have often heard of Kṛṣṇa's *rāsa-līlā* with the cowherd girls in Vṛndāvana. That is not like ordinary exchanges that take place between these material bodies. Rather it is an exchange of feelings through spiritual bodies. One has to be somewhat intelligent to understand this, for a foolish man, who cannot understand what real happiness is, seeks happiness in this material world. In India there is the story of a man who did not know what sugarcane was and was told that it was very sweet to chew. "Oh, what does it look like?" he asked. "It looks just like a bamboo rod," someone said. So the foolish man began to chew all kinds of bamboo rods. How can he begin to experience the sweetness of sugarcane? Similarly, we are trying to get happiness and pleasure, but we are trying for them by chewing this material body; therefore there is no happiness and no pleasure. For the time being there may be some little feeling of pleasure, but that is not actual pleasure, for it is temporary. It is like a show of lightning which we may see flashing in the sky that may momentarily seem like lightning, but the real lightning is beyond that. Because a person does not really know what happiness is, he deviates from real happiness.

The process for establishing oneself in real happiness is this process of Kṛṣṇa consciousness. By Kṛṣṇa consciousness we can gradually develop our real intelligence and naturally enjoy relishing spiritual happiness as we make spiritual progress. As we begin to relish spiritual happiness, we proportionately abandon material happiness. As we make progress in understanding the Absolute Truth, we naturally become detached from this false happiness. If somehow or other one is promoted to that stage of Kṛṣṇa consciousness, what is the result?

yaṁ labdhvā cāparaṁ lābhaṁ
manyate nādhikaṁ tataḥ
yasmin sthito na duḥkhena
guruṇāpi vicālyate

"Upon gaining this, he thinks there is no greater gain. Being situated in such a position, one is never shaken, even in the midst of greatest difficulty." (Bg. 6.22)

When one attains that stage, other achievements appear insignificant. In this material world we are trying to achieve so many things—riches, women, fame, beauty, knowledge, etc.—but as soon as we are situated in Kṛṣṇa consciousness we think, "Oh, no achievement is better than this." Kṛṣṇa consciousness is so potent that a little taste can save one from the greatest danger. As one begins to relish the taste of Kṛṣṇa consciousness, he begins to see other so-called enjoyments and attainments as flat and tasteless. And if one is situated firmly in Kṛṣṇa consciousness, the greatest danger cannot disturb him. There are so many dangers in life because the material world is a place of danger. We tend to close our eyes to this, and because we are foolish we try to adjust to these dangers. We may have many dangerous moments in our lives, but if we are training ourselves in Kṛṣṇa consciousness and preparing ourselves to go home, back to Godhead, we will not care for them. Our attitude will then be: "Dangers come and go—so let them happen." It is very difficult to make this kind of adjustment as long as one is on the materialistic platform and is identifying with the gross body, which is composed of perishable elements. But the more one advances in Kṛṣṇa consciousness, the more he becomes free from bodily designations and this material entanglement.

In *Śrīmad-Bhāgavatam* the material world is compared to a great ocean. Within this material universe there are millions and billions of planets floating in space, and we can just imagine how many Atlantic and Pacific Oceans are there. In fact, the whole material universe is likened to a great ocean of misery, an ocean of birth and death. In order to cross this great ocean of nescience, a strong boat is needed, and that strong boat is the lotus feet of Kṛṣṇa. We should immediately get aboard that boat. We should not hesitate, thinking that Kṛṣṇa's feet are very small. The whole universe is simply resting on His leg. For one who takes shelter of His feet, it is said that the material universe is no more significant than a puddle of water found in the impression of a calf's hoof-print. There is certainly no difficulty in crossing over such a small puddle.

taṁ vidyād duḥkha-saṁyoga-
viyogaṁ yoga-saṁjñitam

"This indeed is actual freedom from all miseries arising from material contact." (Bg. 6.23)

We are entangled in this material world due to uncontrolled senses. The *yoga* process is meant to control these senses. If somehow we can manage to control the senses, we can turn our face to actual spiritual happiness and make our lives successful.

sa niścayena yoktavyo
yogo'nirviṇṇa-cetasā

saṅkalpa-prabhavān kāmāṁs
tyaktvā sarvān aśeṣataḥ
manasaivendriya-grāmaṁ
viniyamya samantataḥ

śanaiḥ śanair uparamed
buddhyā dhṛti-gṛhītayā

ātma-saṁsthaṁ manaḥ kṛtvā
na kiñcid api cintayet

yato yato niścalati
manaś cañcalam asthiram
tatas tato niyamyaitad
ātmany eva vaśaṁ nayet

"One should engage oneself in the practice of *yoga* with undeviating determination and faith. One should abandon, without exception, all material desires born of false ego and thus control all the senses on all sides by the mind. Gradually, step by step, with full conviction, one should become situated in trance by means of intelligence, and thus the mind should be fixed on the Self alone and should think of nothing else. From whatever and wherever the mind wanders due to its flickering and unsteady nature, one must certainly withdraw it and bring it back under the control of the Self."

The mind is always disturbed. It is going sometimes this way and sometimes that way. By *yoga* practice we literally drag the mind to Kṛṣṇa consciousness. The mind strays from Kṛṣṇa consciousness to so many exterior objects because from time immemorial, life after life, that has been our practice. Due to this, there may be great difficulty in the beginning when one tries to fix his mind in Kṛṣṇa consciousness, but these difficulties can all be overcome.

It is because the mind is agitated and not fixed on Kṛṣṇa that it goes from one thought to another. For instance, when we are engaged in work, memories of events that happened ten, twenty, thirty or forty years ago may suddenly come to our mind for no apparent reason. These thoughts come from our subconscious, and because they are always rising, the mind is always agitated. If we agitate a lake or a pond, all the mud from the bottom comes to the surface. Similarly, when the mind is agitated so many thoughts arise from the subconscious that have been stored there over the years. If we do not disturb a pond, the mud will settle to the bottom. This *yoga* process is the means to quiet the mind and allow all these thoughts to settle. For this reason there are so many rules and regulations to follow in order to keep the mind from becoming agitated. If we follow the rules and regulations, gradually the mind will come under control. There are so many don't's and so many do's, and if one is serious about training the mind, he has to follow them. If he acts whimsically, what is the possibility of the mind being controlled? When the mind is finally trained to the point where it will think of nothing but Kṛṣṇa, it will attain peace and will become very tranquil.

praśānta-manasaṁ hy enaṁ
yoginaṁ sukham uttamam
upaiti śānta-rajasaṁ
brahma-bhūtam akalmaṣam

"The *yogī* whose mind is fixed on Me verily attains the highest happiness. By virtue of his identity with Brahman, he is liberated; his mind is peaceful, his passions are quieted, and he is freed from sin." (Bg. 6.27)

The mind is always concocting objects for happiness. I am always thinking, "This will make me happy," or "That will make me happy. Happiness is here. Happiness is there." In this way the mind is taking us anywhere and everywhere. It is as though we are riding on a chariot behind an unbridled horse. We have no power over where we are going but can only sit in horror and watch helplessly. As soon as the mind is engaged in the Kṛṣṇa consciousness process—specifically by chanting Hare Kṛṣṇa, Hare Kṛṣṇa, Kṛṣṇa Kṛṣṇa, Hare Hare/ Hare Rāma, Hare Rāma, Rāma Rāma, Hare Hare—then the wild horses of the mind will gradually come under our control. We must engage in Kṛṣṇa's service every moment of our lives in order to keep the restless and turbulent mind from dragging us from one object to another in a vain search for happiness in the temporary material world.

yuñjann evaṁ sadātmānaṁ
yogī vigata-kalmaṣaḥ
sukhena brahma-saṁsparśam
atyantaṁ sukham aśnute

"Steady in the Self, being freed from all material contamination, the *yogī* achieves the highest perfectional stage of happiness in touch with the supreme consciousness." (Bg. 6.28)

Kṛṣṇa serves as a patron for one who is devoted to Him. When one is in difficulty, his patron saves him. As stated in *Bhagavad-gītā,* Kṛṣṇa is the real friend of every living entity, and we have to revive our friendship with Him. The method for reviving this friendship is the process of Kṛṣṇa consciousness. By practice of Kṛṣṇa consciousness, mundane passionate hankering will come to a stop. This passionate hankering keeps us divorced from Kṛṣṇa. Kṛṣṇa is within us and is waiting for us to turn to Him, but we are too busy passionately eating the fruits of the tree of material desire. This passionate compulsion to enjoy these fruits must stop, and we must situate ourselves in our real identity as Brahman—pure spirit.

2

The Way of Chanting and Knowing Kṛṣṇa

Hare Kṛṣṇa, Hare Kṛṣṇa, Kṛṣṇa Kṛṣṇa, Hare Hare/ Hare Rāma, Hare Rāma, Rāma Rāma, Hare Hare. This is transcendental sound vibration. It will help us to cleanse the dust from the mirror of the mind. At the present moment we have accumulated so much material dust on the mirror of the mind, just as on Second Avenue (New York City) there is dust and soot over everything due to the heavy traffic. Due to our manipulation of material activities, a great deal of dust has collected over our mind's clear mirror, and as a consequence we are unable to see things in perspective. This vibration of transcendental sound (the Hare Kṛṣṇa *mantra*) will cleanse away this dust and enable us to see clearly our real constitutional position. As soon as we come to understand "I am not this body; I am spirit soul, and my symptom is consciousness," we will be able to establish ourselves in real happiness. As our consciousness is purified by this process of chanting Hare Kṛṣṇa, all our material miseries will disappear. There is a fire that is always blazing over this material world, and everyone is trying to extinguish it, but there is no possibility of extinguishing this fire of the miseries of material nature unless we are situated in our pure consciousness, in our spiritual life.

One of the purposes for Lord Kṛṣṇa's descent or appearance in this material world is to extinguish the fire of material existence for all living entities by setting forth the *dharma.*

yadā yadā hi dharmasya
glānir bhavati bhārata
abhyutthānam adharmasya
tadātmānaṁ sṛjāmyaham

paritrāṇāya sādhūnāṁ
vināśāya ca duṣkṛtām
dharma-saṁsthāpanārthāya
sambhavāmi yuge yuge

"Whenever and wherever there is a decline in religious practice, O descendant of Bharata, and a predominant rise of irreligion—at that time I descend Myself. In order to deliver the pious and to annihilate the miscreants, as well as to reestablish the principles of religion, I advent Myself millennium after millennium." (Bg. 4.7-8)

In this verse the word *dharma* is used. This word has been translated into English in various ways. Sometimes it is translated as "faith," but according to Vedic literature, *dharma* is not a kind of faith. Faith may change, but *dharma* cannot be changed. The liquidity of water cannot be changed. If it is changed—if, for instance, water becomes solid—it is actually no longer in its constitutional position. It is existing under a certain qualifying condition. Our *dharma* or constitutional position is that we are part and parcel of the Supreme, and this being the case, we have to dovetail or subjugate our consciousness to the Supreme.

This position of transcendental service to the Supreme Whole is being misused due to material contact. Service is implicit in our constitutional position. Everyone is a servant, and no one is a master. Everyone is serving someone or other. Although the President may be the chief executive of the state, still he is serving the state, and when his services are no longer required, the state disposes of him. To think to oneself, "I am the master of all I survey," is called *māyā,* illusion. Thus in material consciousness our service is being misused under various designations. When we can become free from these designations, that is to say when the dust has been cleared from the mirror of the mind, we will be able to see ourselves in our actual position as eternal servants of Kṛṣṇa.

One should not think that his service in the material world and his service in the spiritual atmosphere are the same. We may shudder to think, "Oh, after liberation will I still be a servant?" This is because we have experience that being a servant in the material world is not very enjoyable, but transcendental service is not like this. In the spiritual world there is no difference between the servant and the master. Here, of course, there is distinction, but in the absolute world everything is one. For instance, in *Bhagavad-gītā* we can see that Kṛṣṇa has taken the position of servant as the chariot driver of Arjuna. In his constitutional position, Arjuna is the servant of Kṛṣṇa, but in behavior we can see that sometimes the Lord becomes the servant of the servant. So we should be careful not to carry materialistic ideas into the spiritual realm. Whatever we have materially experienced is but a perverted reflection of things in spiritual life.

When our constitutional position or *dharma* is deteriorated due to the contaminations of matter, the Lord Himself comes as an incarnation or sends some of His confidential servitors. Lord Jesus Christ called himself the "son of God," and so is a representative of the Supreme. Similarly, Mohammed identified himself as a servant of the Supreme Lord. Thus whenever there is a discrepancy in our constitutional position, the Supreme Lord either comes Himself or sends His representative to inform us of the real position of the living entity.

Therefore, one should not make the mistake of thinking that *dharma* is a created faith. In its proper sense, *dharma* cannot be divorced from the living entity at all. It is to the living entity what sweetness is to sugar, or saltiness is to salt, or solidity is to stone. In no case can it be cut off. The *dharma* of the living entity is to serve, and we can easily see that every living entity has the tendency to serve himself or others. How to serve Kṛṣṇa, how to disentangle ourselves from materialistic service, how to attain Kṛṣṇa consciousness and become free from material designations is all taught as a science by Śrī Kṛṣṇa in *Bhagavad-gītā.*

The word *sādhu* in the verse quoted above, beginning *paritrāṇāya sādhūnām* refers to a holy man or a saintly person. A saintly person is tolerant, very kind to everyone, is a friend to all living entities, is no one's enemy and is always peaceful. There are twenty-six basic qualifications for a holy man, and in the

Bhagavad-gītā we find that Śrī Kṛṣṇa Himself gives the following verdict:

api cet sudurācāro
bhajate mām ananya-bhāk
sādhur eva sa mantavyaḥ
samyag vyavasito hi saḥ

"Even if one commits the most abominable actions, if he is engaged in devotional service, he is to be considered saintly because he is properly situated." (Bg. 9.30)

On the mundane platform, what is morality for one person is immorality for another, and what is immorality for one person is morality for another. According to the Hindu conception, the drinking of wine is immoral, whereas in the Western world, wine drinking is not considered immoral but is a common thing. So morality is dependent on time, place, circumstance, social position, etc. There is, however, a sense of morality and immorality in all societies. In this verse Kṛṣṇa points out that even if one is engaged in immoral acts but at the same time is fully in Kṛṣṇa consciousness, he is to be considered a *sādhu* or a saint. In other words, although a person may have some immoral habits due to his past association, if he is engaged fully in Kṛṣṇa consciousness, these habits are not to be considered important. Whatever the case, if one becomes Kṛṣṇa conscious, he will gradually be purified and will become a *sādhu.* As one progresses in executing Kṛṣṇa consciousness, his bad habits diminish, and he attains to saintly perfection.

In this regard there is the story of a thief who went on a pilgrimage to a holy town, and on route he and the other pilgrims stopped to rest overnight at an inn. Being addicted to stealing, the thief began making plans to steal the other pilgrims' baggage, but he thought, "I'm going on a pilgrimage, so it doesn't seem appropriate that I should steal this baggage. No, I shall not do it." Nonetheless, due to his habit, he could not keep his hands off the baggage. So he picked up one person's bag and placed it in another place, and then another person's bag and placed it elsewhere. He spent all night placing different bags in different places, but his conscience bothered him so that he could not take anything from them. In the morning, when the other pilgrims awoke, they looked around for their bags and couldn't find them. There was a great row, and eventually, one by one, they began to find the bags in various places. After they were all found, the thief explained: "Gentlemen, I am a thief by occupation. Being that I am habituated to stealing at night, I wanted to steal something from your bags, but I thought that since I am going to this holy place, it is not possible to steal. So I may have rearranged the baggage, but please excuse me." This is the characteristic of a bad habit. He does not want to commit theft anymore, but because he is habituated, sometimes he does. Thus Kṛṣṇa says that one who has decided to refrain from his immoral habits and make progress in Kṛṣṇa consciousness is to be considered a *sādhu,* even if out of past habit or by chance he yields to his fault. In the next verse we find that Śrī Kṛṣṇa says:

kṣipraṁ bhavati dharmātmā
śaśvac-chāntiṁ nigacchati
kaunteya pratijānīhi
na me bhaktaḥ praṇaśyati

"He quickly becomes righteous and attains lasting peace. O son of Kuntī, declare it boldly that My devotee never perishes." (Bg. 9.31)

Because one has committed himself to Kṛṣṇa consciousness, it is proclaimed here by Śrī Kṛṣṇa that within a very short time he will become saintly. One may pull the plug out of an electric fan, and the fan may still go on even though the juice has been disconnected, but it is understood that the fan will soon come to a stop. Once we take shelter of the lotus feet of Kṛṣṇa, we turn the switch off for our karmic activities, and although these activities may still revolve, it is to be understood that they will quickly diminish. It is a fact that whoever takes to Kṛṣṇa consciousness does not have to endeavor independently to become a good man. All the good qualifications will automatically come. It is stated in *Śrīmad-Bhāgavatam* that one who has attained Kṛṣṇa consciousness has simultaneously attained all good qualities. On the other hand, if a person is devoid of God consciousness and yet has many good qualities, his good qualities are to be considered useless, for he will not in any way be prohibited from doing that which is undesirable. If one is devoid of Kṛṣṇa consciousness, he is sure to commit mischief in this material world.

janma karma ca me divyam
evaṁ yo vetti tattvataḥ
tyaktvā dehaṁ punar janma
naiti mām eti so 'rjuna

"One who knows the transcendental nature of My appearance and activities does not, upon leaving the body, take his birth again in this material world, but attains My eternal abode, O Arjuna." (Bg. 4.9)

The mission for which Kṛṣṇa appears is here further explained. When He comes with some mission, there are some activities. Of course there are some philosophers who do not believe that God comes as an incarnation. They say, "Why should God come to this rotten world?" But from *Bhagavad-gītā* we understand otherwise. We should always remember that we read *Bhagavad-gītā* as scripture, and whatever is spoken in *Bhagavad-gītā* must be accepted, otherwise there is no reason in reading it. In *Gītā* Kṛṣṇa says that He has come as an incarnation with a mission, and along with His mission there are some activities. We can see, for example, that Kṛṣṇa is active as chariot-driver for Arjuna and engages in so many activities on the battlefield of Kurukṣetra. Just as when there is war one person or nation may side with another person or nation and show partiality, Lord Kṛṣṇa on the battlefield shows some partiality and sides with Arjuna. Actually Kṛṣṇa is not partial to anyone, but externally it appears that He is partial. This partiality, however, should not be accepted in the ordinary sense.

In this verse Kṛṣṇa also points out that His descent into the material world is transcendental. The word *divyam* means transcendental. His activities are not in any way ordinary. Even today, in India, at the end of August the people are accustomed to celebrating Kṛṣṇa's birthday, regardless of sect, just as in the Western world Jesus Christ's birthday is celebrated at Christmas. Kṛṣṇa's birthday is called *Janmāṣṭamī*, and in this verse Kṛṣṇa uses the word *janma* in referring to "My birth." Because there is birth, there are some activities. Kṛṣṇa's birth and activities are transcendental, which means they are not like ordinary births and activities. One may ask how it is that His activities are transcendental. He is born, He takes part in a battle with Arjuna, he has a father by the name of Vasudeva and a mother Devakī and a family —what can be considered transcendental? Kṛṣṇa says, *evaṁ yo vetti tattvataḥ*—we must know of His birth and activities in truth. When one knows of Kṛṣṇa's birth and activities in truth, the result is: *tyaktvā dehaṁ punar janma naiti mām eti so 'rjuna*—when he leaves this material body, he is not born again but goes directly to Kṛṣṇa. This means that he becomes a liberated soul. He goes to the eternal spiritual world and attains his constitutional position full of bliss, knowledge and eternality. All this can be obtained simply by knowing in truth the transcendental nature of Kṛṣṇa's birth and activities.

Ordinarily when one quits the body he has to take up another body. The lives of the living entities are going on simply due to the living entities' changing dress from one body to another—transmigration of the soul—according to the work of the living entities. At the present moment we may think that this material body is our actual body, but it is like a dress. In reality we do have an actual body, a spiritual body. This material body is superficial compared to the real spiritual body of the living entity. When this material body becomes old and worn out, or when it is rendered useless by some accident, we put it aside as we might put aside a soiled or ruined suit and take up another material body.

vāsaṁsi jīrṇāni yathā vihāya
navāni gṛhṇāti naro 'parāṇi
tathā śarīrāṇi vihāya jīrṇāny
anyāni saṁyāti navāni dehī

"As a person puts on new garments, giving up old ones, similarly, the soul accepts new material bodies, giving up the old and useless ones." (Bg. 2.22)

In the beginning the body is the size of a pea. Then it grows to become a baby, then a child, a young boy, a youth, a grown man and an old man, and finally, when it becomes useless, the living entity changes into another body. The body is therefore always changing, and death is simply the ultimate change of the present body.

dehino 'smin yathā dehe
kaumāraṁ yauvanaṁ jarā
tathā dehāntara-prāptir
dhīras tatra na muhyati

"As the embodied soul continually passe
body, from boyhood to youth to old a

similarly passes into another body at death. The self-realized soul is not bewildered by such a change." (Bg. 2.13)

Although the body is changing, the dweller within the body remains the same. Although the boy grows into manhood, the living entity within the body is not changed. It is not that the self who was there as a boy has gone away. Medical science agrees that at every moment the material body is changing. Just as living entities are not bewildered by this, an enlightened man is not bewildered when the body undergoes its ultimate change at death. But a person who does not understand things as they are laments. In the material condition we are simply changing bodies all the time; that is our disease. It is not that we always change to a human body. We may change to an animal body or a demigod body depending on our activities. According to the *Padma Purāṇa* there are 8,400,000 species of life. We can take on any of them at death. But Kṛṣṇa promises that one who knows His birth and activities in truth is freed from this cycle of transmigration.

How does one understand Kṛṣṇa's birth and activities in truth? This is explained in the Eighteenth Chapter of *Bhagavad-gītā:*

bhaktyā mām abhijānāti
yāvān yaś cāsmi tattvataḥ
tato māṁ tattvato jñātvā
viśate tad-anantaram

"One can understand the Supreme Personality as He only by devotional service. And when one is in full consciousness of the Supreme Lord by such devotion, he can enter into the kingdom of God." (Bg. 18.55)

Here again the word *tattvataḥ*, "in truth," is used. One can understand the science of Kṛṣṇa in truth by becoming a devotee. He who is not a devotee, who does not strive for Kṛṣṇa consciousness, cannot understand. At the beginning of the Fourth Chapter also Kṛṣṇa tells Arjuna (Bg. 4.3) that He is explaining this ancient science of *yoga* to him because Arjuna is "My devotee and My friend." For one who simply makes an academic study of *Bhagavad-gītā*, the science of Kṛṣṇa remains a mystery. *Bhagavad-gītā* is not a book that one can just purchase from the bookstore and understand by scholarship alone. Arjuna was not a great scholar, nor a Vedāntist, nor a philosopher nor a *brāhmaṇa*, nor a renunciate; he was a family and military man. But still Kṛṣṇa selected him to be the recipient of *Bhagavad-gītā* and the first authority in the disciplic succession. Why? "Because you are My devotee." That is the qualification to understand *Bhagavad-gītā* as it is and Kṛṣṇa as He is—one must become Kṛṣṇa conscious.

And what is this Kṛṣṇa consciousness? That is the process of cleansing the dust from the mirror of the mind through the chanting of Hare Kṛṣṇa, Hare Kṛṣṇa, Kṛṣṇa Kṛṣṇa, Hare Hare/ Hare Rāma, Hare Rāma, Rāma Rāma, Hare Hare. By chanting this *mantra* and by hearing *Bhagavad-gītā*, we can gradually attain to Kṛṣṇa consciousness. *Īśvaraḥ sarva-bhūtānām*—Kṛṣṇa is always present within our heart. The individual soul and the Supersoul are both sitting in the tree of the body. The individual soul *(jīva)* is eating the fruit of the tree, and the Supersoul (Paramātmā) is witnessing. As the individual soul begins the process of devotional service and gradually begins to develop his Kṛṣṇa consciousness, the Supersoul who is seated within begins to help him dust all the impurities from the mirror of the mind. Kṛṣṇa is a friend to all saintly persons, and the attempt to become Kṛṣṇa conscious is a saintly endeavor. *Śravaṇaṁ kīrtanam*—by chanting and hearing one can come to understand the science of Kṛṣṇa and thereby come to understand Kṛṣṇa. And upon understanding Kṛṣṇa, one can, at the moment of death, go immediately to His abode in the spiritual world. This spiritual world is described thus in *Bhagavad-gītā:*

na tad bhāsayate sūryo
na śaśāṅko na pāvakaḥ
yad gatvā na nivartante
tad dhāma paramaṁ mama

"That abode of Mine is not illumined by the sun or moon, nor by electricity. One who reaches it never returns to this material world." (Bg. 15.6)

This material world is always dark; therefore we require the sun, moon and electricity. The *Vedas* enjoin us not to remain in this darkness but to transfer ourselves to the world of illumination, the spiritual world. The word darkness has a twofold meaning; it not only means without light, but it means ignorance.

The Supreme Lord has manifold energies. It is not that he comes to this material world to perform activities. It is stated in the *Vedas* that the Supreme Lord has nothing to do. In *Bhagavad-gītā* Śrī Kṛṣṇa also says:

na me pārthāsti kartavyaṁ
triṣu lokeṣu kiñcana
nānavāptam avāptavyaṁ
varta eva ca karmaṇi

"O son of Pṛthā, there is no work prescribed for Me within all the three planetary systems. Nor am I in want of anything, nor have I need to obtain anything—and yet I am engaged in work." (Bg. 3.22)

We should therefore not think that Kṛṣṇa is required to descend upon this material world and engage in so many activities. No one is equal to or greater than Kṛṣṇa, and He has all knowledge naturally. It is not that He has to undergo penances to acquire knowledge or that He at any time has to receive knowledge or attain knowledge. At all times and in all conditions He is full of knowledge. He may be speaking *Bhagavad-gītā* to Arjuna, but at no time was He ever taught *Bhagavad-gītā*. One who can understand that this is Kṛṣṇa's position does not have to return to the cycle of birth and death in this material world. Being under the influence of illusion, we spend our lifetimes trying to make adjustments to this material atmosphere, but this is not the purpose of human life. Human life is meant for understanding the science of Kṛṣṇa.

Our material needs are these: the problem of eating, of mating, of sleeping, of defending ourselves and of acquiring sense gratification. These are common both to human beings and to animals. The animals are busily engaged trying to solve these problems, and if we are also only engaged in solving them how are we any different from the animals? The human being, however, has a special qualification whereby he can develop transcendental Kṛṣṇa consciousness, but if he does not avail himself of this, he is in the animal category. The defect of modern civilization is that it puts too much stress on solving these survival problems. As spiritual living beings it is incumbent upon us to extricate ourselves from this entanglement of birth and death. We should therefore be careful not to miss the special opportunity of human life. Śrī Kṛṣṇa Himself comes to deliver *Bhagavad-gītā* and to help us to become God conscious. Indeed, this very material creation is given to us to utilize for this cultivation. But if after receiving this chance and this gift of human life we do not utilize them to develop Kṛṣṇa consciousness, we shall be missing this rare opportunity. The process for cultivation is very simple: *śravaṇam kīrtanam*—hearing and chanting. We have nothing to do other than listen, and by listening carefully, enlightenment is sure to come. Kṛṣṇa will surely help, for He is seated within. We only have to make the effort and spare a little time. We will not need anyone to ask us whether we are making progress. We will know it automatically, just as a hungry man knows that he has been satisfied by a full meal.

Actually this process of Kṛṣṇa consciousness or self-realization is not very difficult. Kṛṣṇa taught it to Arjuna in *Bhagavad-gītā,* and if we understand *Bhagavad-gītā* just as Arjuna did, we will have no problem in coming to the perfectional state. But if we try to interpret *Bhagavad-gītā* according to our own mundane academic mentality, we spoil it all.

As stated before, this chanting of Hare Kṛṣṇa is a process by which all contaminations due to material association are removed from the mirror of the mind. There is no need for external help in reviving our Kṛṣṇa consciousness, for Kṛṣṇa consciousness is dormant within the self. In fact, it is the very quality of the self. We have only to invoke it by this process. Kṛṣṇa consciousness is an eternal fact. It is not a doctrine or set of beliefs imposed by some organization. It is within all living entities, whether they be human being or animal. When Lord Caitanya Mahāprabhu was passing through the jungles of South India some five hundred years ago, He chanted Hare Kṛṣṇa, and all the animals—the tigers, elephants and deer—joined Him in dancing to the holy names. Of course this depends on the purity of the chanting. As we progress in chanting, purification is sure to come.

3
Seeing Kṛṣṇa Everywhere and Always

In our practical life, Kṛṣṇa instructs us how to invoke Kṛṣṇa consciousness. It is not that we are to stop executing our duty or to cease from activity. Rather, activities have to be conducted in Kṛṣṇa consciousness. Everyone has a vocation in life, but with what consciousness does he enter upon it? Everyone is thinking, "Oh, I must have a vocation in order to maintain my family." Society, the government or the family have to be satisfied, and no one is free from such consciousness. One has to be in proper consciousness to execute any activity nicely. He whose consciousness is agitated, who is like a madman, cannot execute any duty. We should execute our duty properly, but we should do it thinking to satisfy Kṛṣṇa. It is not that we have to change our process of work, but we do have to understand for whom we are working. Whatever activity we have to do we must execute, but we should not be carried away by *kāma,* desire. The Sanskrit word *kāma* is used to indicate lust, desire or sense satisfaction. Śrī Kṛṣṇa instructs that we should not work for the satisfaction of *kāma* or our own lust. The whole teaching of *Bhagavad-gītā* is based on this principle.

Arjuna wanted to satisfy his senses by refraining from fighting with his relatives, but Kṛṣṇa spoke to him to convince him to execute his duty for the satisfaction of the Supreme. Materially it may seem very pious that he is giving up his claim for a kingdom and refusing to kill his relatives, but Kṛṣṇa did not approve of this because the principle for Arjuna's decision was to satisfy his own senses. One's business or occupation need not be changed—as Arjuna's was not changed—but one does have to change his consciousness. In order to change this consciousness, however, knowledge is required. That knowledge is knowing "I am part and parcel of Kṛṣṇa, the superior energy of Kṛṣṇa." That is real knowledge. Relative knowledge may teach us how to repair a machine, but real knowledge is knowing our position as being integral with Kṛṣṇa. Being part of Him, our pleasure, which is partial, is dependent on the whole. For instance, my hand can take pleasure when it is attached to my body and serves it. It does not take pleasure in serving another's body. Because we are part of Kṛṣṇa, our pleasure is in serving Him. "I cannot be happy serving you," everyone is thinking. "I can only be happy serving myself." But no one knows who the self is. That self is Kṛṣṇa.

mamaivāṁśo jīva-loke
jīva-bhūtaḥ sanātanaḥ
manaḥ ṣaṣṭhānīndriyāṇi
prakṛti-sthāni karṣati

"The living entities in this conditioned world are My eternal, fragmental parts. Due to conditioned life, they are struggling very hard with the six senses, which include the mind." (Bg. 15.7)

The *jīvas,* or living entities, are now detached from the whole due to material contact. It is therefore necessary for us to strive to attach ourselves again through the latent Kṛṣṇa consciousness that is within us. Artificially, we are trying to forget Kṛṣṇa and live independently, but this is not possible. When we strive to live independent of Kṛṣṇa, we come under the influence of the laws of material nature. If one thinks he is independent of Kṛṣṇa, he becomes dependent on the illusory energy of Kṛṣṇa, just as if one thinks that he is independent of the government and its regulations, he becomes dependent on the police force. Everyone is trying to become independent, and this is called *māyā*, illusion. Individually, communally, socially, nationally, or universally, it is not possible to become independent. When we come to realize that we are dependent, we will have attained knowledge. Today so many people are striving for peace in the world, but they do not know how to implement that peace formula. The United Nations has been striving for peace for so many years, but still war is going on.

yac cāpi sarva-bhūtānāṁ
bījaṁ tad aham arjuna
na tad asti vinā yat syān
mayā bhūtaṁ carācaram

"Furthermore, O Arjuna, I am the generating seed of all existences. There is no being—moving or unmoving—that can exist without Me." (Bg. 10.39)

Kṛṣṇa is thus the proprietor of everything, the ultimate beneficiary and the receiver of the results of everything. We may consider ourselves to be the proprietors of the fruits of our labor, but this is a misconception. We must come to understand that Kṛṣṇa is the ultimate proprietor of the fruits of all our works. Hundreds of people may be working in an office, but they understand that whatever profit the business makes belongs to the proprietor. As soon as a teller at the bank thinks, "Oh, I have so much money. I am the proprietor. Let me take it home with me," his trouble begins. If we think that we can use whatever wealth we have amassed for our own sense gratification, we are acting out of *kāma,* lust. But if we come to understand that everything we have belongs to Kṛṣṇa, we are liberated. We may have the same money in our hands, but as soon as we think that we are the proprietor, we are under the influence of *māyā.* One who is situated in the consciousness that everything belongs to Kṛṣṇa is an actual learned man.

īśāvāsyam idaṁ sarvaṁ
yat kiñca jagatyāṁ jagat
tena tyaktena bhuñjīthā
mā gṛdhaḥ kasya svid dhanam

"Everything animate or inanimate that is within the universe is controlled and owned by the Lord. One should therefore accept only those things necessary for himself, which are set aside as his quota, and one must not accept other things, knowing well to whom they belong." (*Śrī Īśopaniṣad, Mantra* 1)

This consciousness of *īśāvāsya*—everything belongs to Kṛṣṇa—must be revived, not only individually but nationally and universally. Then there will be peace. We often tend to be philanthropic and altruistic, and we strive to be friends with our countrymen, with our families and with all the peoples of the world—but this is based on a wrong conception. The real friend is Kṛṣṇa, and if we want to benefit our family, nation or planet, we will work for Him. If we have our family's welfare in mind, we will try to make all members Kṛṣṇa conscious. There are so many men trying to benefit their families, but unfortunately they do not succeed. They do not know what the real problem is. As the *Bhāgavatam* says, one should not attempt to become a father, or mother, or teacher unless he is able to save his children from death, from the grip of material nature. The father should be in knowledge of Kṛṣṇa, and he should be determined that the innocent children who are entrusted to him will not have to undergo the cycle of birth and death again. He should be resolved to train his children in such a way that they will no longer have to be subjected to the painful cycle of birth and death. But before one can do this, he has to make himself expert. If he becomes expert in Kṛṣṇa consciousness, he can help not only his children but his society and nation. But if he himself is bound by ignorance, how can he unite others who are similarly bound? Before one can make others free, he must be free himself. Actually no one is a free man, for everyone is under the spell of material nature, but one who is surrendered to Kṛṣṇa cannot be touched by *māyā.* He, of all men, is free. If one places himself in sunlight, there is no question of darkness. But if one places himself in artificial light, it may flicker and go out. Kṛṣṇa is just like sunlight. Where He is present, there is no question of darkness and ignorance. The wise men, the *mahātmās,* understand this.

ahaṁ sarvasya prabhavo
mattaḥ sarvaṁ pravartate
iti matvā bhajante māṁ
budhā bhāva-samanvitāḥ

"I am the source of all spiritual and material worlds. Everything emanates from Me. The wise who know this perfectly engage in My devotional service and worship Me with all their hearts." (Bg. 10.8)

In this verse the word *budha* is used, which indicates a wise man or one who is learned. What is his symptom? He knows that Kṛṣṇa is the fountainhead of everything, of all emanations. He knows that whatever he sees is but an emanation of Kṛṣṇa. In the material world, sex life is the most prominent factor. Sexual attraction is found in all species of life, and one may ask where it comes from. The wise man understands that this tendency is in Kṛṣṇa and that it is revealed in His relationships with the damsels of Vraja. Whatever is found in this material world can also be found in perfection in Kṛṣṇa. The difference is that in the material world everything is manifest in a perverted form. In Kṛṣṇa all of these tendencies and manifestations exist in pure consciousness, in spirit. One who knows this, in full knowledge, becomes a pure devotee of Kṛṣṇa.

mahātmānas tu māṁ pārtha
daivīṁ prakṛtim āśritāḥ
bhajanty ananya-manaso
jñātvā bhūtādim avyayam

satataṁ kīrtayanto māṁ
yatantaś ca dṛḍha-vratāḥ
namasyantaś ca māṁ bhaktyā
nitya-yuktā upāsate

"O son of Pṛthā, those who are not deluded, the great souls, are under the protection of the divine nature. They are fully engaged in devotional service because they know Me as the Supreme Personality of Godhead, original and inexhaustible. Always chanting My glories, endeavoring with great determination, bowing down before Me, these great souls perpetually worship Me with devotion."(Bg.9.13-14).

Who is the great soul, the *mahātmā?* It is he who is under the influence of the superior energy. At present we are under the influence of Kṛṣṇa's inferior energy. As living entities, our position is marginal—we can transfer ourselves to either of the two energies. Kṛṣṇa is fully independent, and because we are part and parcel of Him we also have this quality of independence. Therefore we have a choice as to which energy we will function under. Because we are ignorant of the superior nature, we have no alternative but to remain in the inferior nature.

Some philosophies propound that there is no nature other than the one we are presently experiencing and that the only solution to this is to nullify it and become void. But we cannot be void because we are living entities. It does not mean that we are finished just because we change our bodies. Before we can get out from the influence of material nature, we have to understand where our place actually is, where we are to go. If we do not know where to go, then we will simply say, "Oh, we do not know what is superior and inferior. All we know is this, so let us stay here and rot." *Bhagavad-gītā*, however, gives us information of the superior energy, the superior nature.

What Kṛṣṇa speaks, He speaks for all eternity; it does not change. It does not matter what our present occupation is or what Arjuna's occupation was—we only have to change our consciousness. At present we are guided by the consciousness of self-interest, but we do not know what our real self-interest is. Actually we do not have self-interest, but sense interest. Whatever we are doing, we are doing to satisfy the senses. It is this consciousness that has to be changed. In its place we must implant our real self-interest—Kṛṣṇa consciousness.

How is this done? How is it possible to become Kṛṣṇa conscious in every step of our life? Actually Kṛṣṇa makes it very easy for us:

raso 'ham apsu kaunteya
prabhāsmi śaśi-sūryayoḥ
praṇavaḥ sarva-vedeṣu
śabdaḥ khe pauruṣaṁ nṛṣu

"O son of Kuntī [Arjuna], I am the taste of water, the light of the sun and the moon, the syllable *om* in the Vedic *mantras;* I am the sound in ether and ability in man." (Bg. 7.8)

In this verse Śrī Kṛṣṇa is describing how we can become Kṛṣṇa conscious fully, in all stages of life.

All living entities must drink water. The taste of water is so nice that when we are thirsty nothing but water seems to do. No manufacturer can create the pure taste of water. We can thus remember Kṛṣṇa or God when we drink water. No one can avoid drinking water every day of his life, so God consciousness is there—how can we forget?

Similarly, when there is some illumination, that is also Kṛṣṇa. The original effulgence in the spiritual sky, the *brahmajyoti,* emanates from the body of Kṛṣṇa. This material sky is covered. The very nature of the material universe is darkness, which we experience at night. It is being artificially illuminated by the sun, by the reflected light of the moon, and by electricity. Where is this illumination coming from? The sun is being illumined by the *brahmajyoti,* or the bright effulgence of the spiritual world. In the spiritual world there is no need for sun, moon or electricity because there everything is illuminated by the *brahmajyoti.* On this earth, however, we can remember Kṛṣṇa whenever we see some illumination from the sun.

When we chant the Vedic *mantras* which begin with *om,* we can also remember Kṛṣṇa. *Om,* like Hare Kṛṣṇa, is also an address to God, and *om* is also Kṛṣṇa. *Śabdaḥ* means sound, and whenever we hear any sound we should know that it is a vibration of the original sound, the pure spiritual sound *om* or Hare Kṛṣṇa. Whatever sound we hear in the material world is but a reflection of that original spiritual sound *om.* In this way when we hear sound, when we drink water, when we see some illumination, we can remember God. If we can do this, then when will we not remember God? This is the process of Kṛṣṇa consciousness. In this way we can remember Kṛṣṇa twenty-four hours a day, and in this way Kṛṣṇa is with us. Of course Kṛṣṇa is always with us, but as soon as we remember this, His presence is factual and is felt.

There are nine different processes for associating with God, and the first method of association is *śravaṇam*—hearing. By reading *Bhagavad-gītā* we hear the speeches of Śrī Kṛṣṇa, which means that we are actually associating with Kṛṣṇa or God. (We should always remember that when we speak of Kṛṣṇa, we refer to God.) Inasmuch as we associate with God and as we go on hearing the words of Kṛṣṇa and His names, the contamination of material nature is reduced. In understanding that Kṛṣṇa is sound, illumination, water, and so many other things, it becomes impossible to avoid Kṛṣṇa. If we can remember Kṛṣṇa in this way, our association with Him is permanent.

Association with Kṛṣṇa is like association with sunshine. Where there is sunshine, there is no contamination. As long as one is out in the ultraviolet rays of the sun, he will not be diseased. In western medicine, sunshine is recommended for all kinds of diseases, and according to the *Vedas* a diseased man should worship the sun for cure. Similarly, if we associate with Kṛṣṇa in Kṛṣṇa consciousness, our maladies are cured. By chanting Hare Kṛṣṇa we can associate with Kṛṣṇa, and we can see the water as Kṛṣṇa, the sun and the moon as Kṛṣṇa, and we can hear Kṛṣṇa in sound and taste Him in water. Unfortunately, in our present condition we have forgotten Kṛṣṇa. But now we have to revive our spiritual life by remembering Him.

This process of *śravaṇaṁ kīrtanam*—hearing and chanting—was approved by Lord Caitanya Mahāprabhu. When Lord Caitanya was speaking with Rāmānanda Rāya, a friend of the Lord's and a great devotee, the Lord questioned him about the methods of spiritual realization. Rāmānanda recommended *varṇāśrama-dharma, sannyāsa,* the renunciation of work, and so many other methods, but Lord Caitanya said, "No, all of these are not so good." Each time Rāmānanda Rāya suggested something, Lord Caitanya rejected it, requesting a better method for spiritual development. Finally Rāmānanda Rāya quoted a Vedic aphorism which recommended that one give up all unnecessary endeavor in mental speculation for understanding God because by speculation it is not possible to arrive at the ultimate truth. Scientists, for instance, may speculate about distant stars and planets, but they can never come to any conclusions without experience. One may go on speculating throughout his life and never reach any conclusions.

It is especially useless to speculate about God. Therefore *Śrīmad-Bhāgavatam* recommends that all sorts of speculation should be given up. It is recommended instead that one become submissive, realizing that not only is he an insignificant creature, but that this earth is only one small point in the great universe. New York City may seem very large, but when one realizes that the earth is such a small spot, and that on the earth the United States is just another small spot, and that in the United States New York City is but a small spot, and that in New York the individual is only one out of millions, then one can understand that he is not so very important after all. Realizing our insignificance in the face of the universe and God, we should not be artificially puffed-up but should be submissive. We should be very careful not to fall prey to the frog philosophy. Once there was a frog in a well, and upon being informed of the existence of the Atlantic Ocean by a friend, he asked the friend, "Oh, what is this Atlantic Ocean?"

"It is a vast body of water," his friend replied.

"How vast? Is it double the size of this well?"

"Oh no, much much larger," his friend replied.

"How much larger? Ten times the size?" In this way the frog went on calculating. But what is the possibility of his ever understanding the depths and far reaches of the great ocean? Our faculties, experience, and powers of speculation are always limited. We can only give rise to such frog philosophy. Therefore *Śrīmad-Bhāgavatam* recommends that we give up the method of speculation as a waste of time in trying to understand the Supreme.

After giving up speculation, what should we do? *Bhāgavatam* recommends that we become submissive and hear the message of God submissively. This message may be found also in the *Bhagavad-gītā* and other Vedic literatures, in the Bible or the Koran—in any bona fide scripture—or it may be heard from a realized soul. The main point is that one should not speculate but should simply hear about God. What will be the result of such hearing? Regardless of what one is—whether he be a poor or rich man, an American, European or Indian, a *brāhmaṇa, śūdra* or whatever—if one but hears the transcendental word of God, the Lord, who can never be conquered by any power or force, will be conquered by love. Arjuna was a friend of Kṛṣṇa's, but Kṛṣṇa, although the Supreme Godhead, became Arjuna's chariot driver, a menial servant. Arjuna loved Kṛṣṇa, and Kṛṣṇa reciprocated his love in this way. Similarly, when Kṛṣṇa was a child, He playfully took the shoes of His father, Nanda Mahārāja, and put them on His head. People may try very hard to become one with God, but actually we can surpass that—we can become father of God. Of course God is the father of all creatures, and He has no father Himself, but He accepts His devotee, His lover, as a father. Kṛṣṇa agrees to be conquered by His devotee out of love. All one has to do is hear the message of the Lord very carefully.

In the Seventh Chapter of *Bhagavad-gītā* Śrī Kṛṣṇa gives additional ways in which He can be perceived in every step of life:

puṇyo gandhaḥ pṛthivyāṁ ca
tejaś cāsmi vibhāvasau
jīvanaṁ sarva-bhūteṣu
tapaś cāsmi tapasviṣu

"I am the original fragrance of the earth, and I am the heat in fire. I am the life of all that lives, and I am the penances of all ascetics." (Bg. 7.9)

The words *puṇyo gandhaḥ* refer to fragrances. Only Kṛṣṇa can create flavors and fragrances. We may synthetically create some scents or fragrances, but these are not as good as the originals that occur in nature. When we smell a good natural fragrance, we can think, "Oh, here is God. Here is Kṛṣṇa." Or when we see some natural beauty, we can think, "Oh, here is Kṛṣṇa." Or when we see something uncommon, powerful or wonderful, we can think, "Here is Kṛṣṇa." Or when we see any form of life, whether it be in a tree, in a plant, or an animal or in a human being, we should understand that this life is part and parcel of Kṛṣṇa, for as soon as the spiritual spark, which is part and parcel of Kṛṣṇa, is taken away from the body, the body disintegrates.

bījaṁ māṁ sarva-bhūtānāṁ
viddhi pārtha sanātanam
buddhir buddhimatām asmi
tejas tejasvinām aham

"O son of Pṛthā, know that I am the original seed of all existences, the intelligence of the intelligent, and the prowess of all powerful men." (Bg. 7.10)

Here again it is explicitly stated that Kṛṣṇa is the life of all that lives. Thus at every step we can see God. People may ask, "Can you show me God?" Yes, of course. God can be seen in so many ways. But if one closes his eyes and says, "I shall not see God," then how can He be shown?

In the above verse the word *bījam* means seed, and that seed is proclaimed to be eternal *(sanātanam)*. One may see a huge tree, but what is the origin of this tree? It is the seed, and that seed is eternal. The seed of existence is within every living entity. The body itself may go through so many changes—it may develop within the mother's womb, come out as a small baby and grow through childhood and adulthood—but the seed of that existence that is within is permanent. Therefore it is *sanātanam.* Imperceivably we are changing our bodies at every moment, at every second. But the *bījam,* the seed, the spiritual spark, does not change. Kṛṣṇa proclaims Himself to be this eternal seed within all existences. He is also the intelligence of an intelligent person. Without being favored by Kṛṣṇa, one cannot become extraordinarily intelligent. Everyone is trying to be more intelligent than others, but without the favor of Kṛṣṇa this is not possible. Therefore whenever we encounter someone with extraordinary intelligence we should think, "That intelligence is Kṛṣṇa." Similarly, the influence of one who is very influential is also Kṛṣṇa.

balaṁ balavatāṁ cāhaṁ
kāma-rāga-vivarjitam
dharmāviruddho bhūteṣu
kāmo 'smi bharatarṣabha

"I am the strength of the strong, devoid of passion and desire. I am sex life which is not contrary to religious principles, O Lord of the Bharatas [Arjuna]." (Bg. 7.11)

The elephant and the gorilla are very strong animals, and we should understand that they get their strength from Kṛṣṇa. The human being cannot acquire such strength by his own endeavor, but if Kṛṣṇa so favors, a man can get strength to exceed the elephant thousands of times. The great warrior Bhīma, who fought in the battle of Kurukṣetra, was said to have strength ten thousand times that of an elephant. Similarly, desire or lust *(kāma)* which is not against religious principles should also be seen as Kṛṣṇa. What is this lust? Lust generally means sex life, but here *kāma* refers to sex life which is not against religious principles, that is to say, sex for the begetting of good children. If one can beget good Kṛṣṇa conscious children, he can have sex thousands of times, but if he can only beget children who are raised in the consciousness of cats and dogs, his sex life is to be considered irreligious. In religious and civilized societies, marriage is intended as an indication that a couple is to engage in sex for begetting good children. Therefore married sex life is considered religious, and unmarried sex life is considered irreligious. Actually there is no difference between the *sannyāsī* and the householder provided that the householder's sexual activities are based on religious principles.

ye caiva sāttvikā bhāvā
rājasās tāmasāś ca ye
matta eveti tān viddhi
na tv ahaṁ teṣu te mayi

"All states of being—be they of goodness, passion or ignorance—are manifested by My energy. I am, in one sense, everything—but I am independent. I am not under the modes of this material nature." (Bg. 7.12)

One may question Kṛṣṇa in this way: "You say You are sound, water, illumination, fragrance, the seed of all, strength, and *kāma,* desire—does that mean that you exist simply in the mode of goodness?" In the material world there are the modes of goodness, passion and ignorance. Thus far, Kṛṣṇa has described Himself as that which is good (for instance, sex in marriage according to religious principles). But what about the other modes? Does not Kṛṣṇa exist in them? In answer, Kṛṣṇa replies that whatever is seen in the material world is due to an interaction of three modes of material nature. Whatever can be observed is a combination of goodness, passion or ignorance, and in all cases these three states are "produced by Me." Because they are produced by Kṛṣṇa, their position is in Him, but He is not in them, for Kṛṣṇa Himself is transcendental to the three modes. Thus, in another sense, bad and evil things, which are produced out of ignorance, are also Kṛṣṇa, when they are applied by Kṛṣṇa. How is this? For example, an electrical engineer is producing electrical energy. In our homes we are experiencing this electrical energy as coldness in the refrigerator or heat in the electric stove, but at the power plant electrical energy is neither cold nor hot. The manifestations of this energy may be different for the living entities, but for Kṛṣṇa they are not different. Therefore Kṛṣṇa sometimes acts on what appears to be the principles of passion or ignorance, but for Kṛṣṇa there is nothing but Kṛṣṇa, just as for the electrical engineer electrical energy is simply electricity and nothing else. He makes no distinction that this is "cold electricity" or that is "hot electricity."

Everything is being generated by Kṛṣṇa. Indeed, the *Vedānta-sūtra* confirms: *athāto brahma-jijñāsā janmādy asya yataḥ:* everything is flowing from the

Supreme Absolute Truth. What the living entity is considering to be bad or good is only so for the living entity, for he is conditioned. But because Kṛṣṇa is not conditioned, for Him there is no question of bad or good. Because we are conditioned, we are suffering from dualities, but for Him everything is perfect.

4

The Roads of the Foolish and the Wise

Kṛṣṇa is thus explaining Himself as He is. Yet we are not attracted to Him. Why is this? The reason is given by Kṛṣṇa Himself:

daivī hy eṣā guṇamayī
mama māyā duratyayā
mām eva ye prapadyante
māyām etāṁ taranti te

"This divine energy of Mine, consisting of the three modes of material nature, is difficult to overcome. But those who have surrendered unto Me can easily cross beyond it." (Bg. 7.14)

The material world is pervaded by the three qualities of material nature. All living entities are influenced by these qualities. If they are primarily influenced by the mode of goodness, they are called *brāhmaṇas,* and if they are influenced by the mode of passion, they are called *kṣatriyas.* If they are influenced by the modes of passion and ignorance, they are *vaiṣyas,* and if they are influenced by ignorance, they are *śūdras.* This is not an artificial imposition due to birth or social status but is according to *guṇa,* or the mode of nature under which one is operating.

cātur-varṇyaṁ mayā sṛṣṭaṁ
guṇa-karma-vibhāgaśaḥ

tasya kartāram api māṁ
viddhy akartāram avyayam

"According to the three modes of material nature and the work ascribed to them, the four divisions of human society were created by Me. And, although I am the creator of this system, you should know that I am yet the non-doer, being unchangeable." (Bg. 4.13)

It is not that this system refers to the perverted caste system in India. Śrī Kṛṣṇa specifically states: *guṇa-karma-vibhāgaśaḥ:* men are classified according to the *guṇa* or the mode under which they are operating, and this applies to men all over the universe. When Kṛṣṇa speaks, we must understand that whatever He says is not limited but is universally true. He claims to be the father of all living entities—even the animals, the aquatics, the trees, plants, worms, birds and bees are all claimed to be His sons. Śrī Kṛṣṇa asserts that the entire universe is illusioned by the interactions of the three qualities of material nature, and we are under the spell of that illusion; therefore we cannot understand what God is.

What is the nature of this illusion, and how can it be overcome? That is also explained in *Bhagavad-gītā:*

daivī hy eṣā guṇamayī
mama māyā duratyayā
mām eva ye prapadyante
māyām etāṁ taranti te

"This divine energy of Mine, consisting of the three modes of material nature, is difficult to overcome.

But those who have surrendered to Me can easily cross beyond it." (Bg. 7.14)

No one can get rid of the entanglement of the three qualities of material nature by mental speculation. The three *guṇas* are very strong and hard to overcome. Can't we feel how we are in the grip of material nature? The word *guṇa* (mode) also means rope. When someone is bound by three strong ropes, he is certainly very tightly secured. Our hands and legs are all bound by the strong ropes of goodness, passion and ignorance. Are we therefore to abandon hope? No, for here Śrī Kṛṣṇa promises that whoever surrenders unto Him is at once free. When one becomes Kṛṣṇa conscious—whether in this way or that way—he becomes free.

We are all related to Kṛṣṇa, for we are all His sons. A son may have a disagreement with his father, but it is not possible for him to break that relation. In the course of his life he will be asked who he is, and he will have to reply, "I am the son of so and so." That relation cannot be broken. We are all sons of God, and that relationship with Him is eternal, but we have simply forgotten. Kṛṣṇa is all-powerful, all-famous, all-wealthy, all-beautiful, all-knowledgeable, and He is full of renunciation as well. Although we are friends of such a great personality, we have forgotten it. If a rich man's son forgets his father, leaves home and becomes mad, he may lie on the street to go to sleep, or he may beg money for food, but all of this is due to his forgetfulness. If someone, however, gives him information that he is simply suffering because he has left his father's home and that his father, a very wealthy man and owner of vast property, is anxious to have him return—the person is a great benefactor.

In this material world we are always suffering under threefold miseries—the miseries arising from the body and the mind, from other living entities, and from natural catastrophes. Being covered by illusion, by the modes of material nature, we do not take account of these miseries. However, we should always know that in the material world we are undergoing so much suffering. One who has sufficiently developed consciousness, who is intelligent, inquires why he is suffering. "I do not want miseries. Why am I suffering?" When this question arises, there is chance for becoming Kṛṣṇa conscious.

As soon as we surrender ourselves to Kṛṣṇa, He welcomes us very cordially. It is just like a lost child who returns to his father and says, "My dear father, due to some misunderstanding I left your protection, but I have suffered. Now I return to you." The father embraces his son and says, "My dear boy, come on. I was so anxious for you all the days you were gone, and now I'm so happy you have come back." The father is so kind. We are in the same position. We have to surrender to Kṛṣṇa, and it is not very difficult. When the son surrenders to the father, is it a very difficult job? It is very natural, and the father is always waiting to receive the son. There is no question of insult. If we bow down before our Supreme Father and touch His feet, there is no harm for us, nor is it difficult. Indeed, it is glorious for us. Why should we not? By surrendering unto

Kṛṣṇa we come immediately under His protection and are relieved of all miseries. This is validated by all scriptures. At the end of *Bhagavad-gītā,* Śrī Kṛṣṇa says:

sarva-dharmān parityajya
mām ekaṁ śaraṇaṁ vraja
ahaṁ tvāṁ sarva-pāpebhyo
mokṣayiṣyāmi mā śucaḥ

"Abandon all varieties of religion and just surrender unto Me. I shall deliver you from all sinful reaction. Do not fear." (Bg. 18.66)

When we throw ourselves at the feet of God, we come under His protection, and from that time on there is no fear for us. When children are under the protection of their parents, they are fearless because they know that their parents will not let them be harmed. *Mām eva ye prapadyante:* Kṛṣṇa promises that those who surrender to Him have no cause for fear.

If surrender unto Kṛṣṇa is such an easy thing, then why don't people do it? Instead there are many who are challenging the very existence of God, claiming that nature and science are everything and that God is nothing. So-called advancement of civilization in knowledge means that the populace is becoming more mad. Instead of being cured, the disease is being increased. People don't care for God, but they care for nature, and it is nature's business to give kicks in the form of the threefold miseries. She is always administering these kicks twenty-four hours a day. However, we have become so accustomed to being kicked that we think it is all right and consider it to be the ordinary course of things. We have become very proud of our education, but we tell material nature, "Thank you very much for kicking me. Now please continue." Thus deluded, we think that we have even conquered material nature. But how is this so? Nature is still inflicting upon us the miseries of birth, old age, disease and death. Has any one solved these problems? Then what advancement have we really made in knowledge and civilization? We are under the stringent rules of material nature, but still we are thinking that we have conquered. This is called *māyā.*

There may be some difficulty in surrendering to the father of this body, for he has limited knowledge and power, but Kṛṣṇa is not like an ordinary father. Kṛṣṇa is unlimited and has full knowledge, full power, full wealth, full beauty, full fame and full renunciation. Shouldn't we consider ourselves lucky to go to such a father and enjoy His property? Yet no one seems to care about this, and now everyone is making propaganda that there is no God. Why do people not seek Him out? The answer is given in the next verse of *Bhagavad-gītā:*

na māṁ duṣkṛtino mūḍhāḥ
prapadyante narādhamāḥ
māyayāpahṛta-jñānā
āsuraṁ bhāvam āśritāḥ

"Those miscreants who are grossly foolish, lowest among mankind, whose knowledge is stolen by illusion, and who partake of the atheistic nature of demons, do not surrender unto Me." (Bg. 7.15)

In this way the fools are categorized. A *duṣkṛtī* is always acting against the scriptural injunctions. The business of current civilization is to break scriptural rules—that's all. By definition, a pious man is one who doesn't. There must be some standard to distinguish between *duṣkṛtī* (an evil doer) and *sukṛtī* (a virtuous man). Every civilized country has some scripture—it may be Christian, Hindu, Moslem or Buddhist. That doesn't matter. The point is that the book of authority, the scripture, is there. One who does not follow its injunctions is considered an outlaw.

Another category mentioned in this verse is *mūḍha,* fool number one. The *narādhama* is one who is low in the human scale, and *māyayāpahṛta-jñāna* refers to one whose knowledge is carried away by *māyā,* or illusion. *Āsuraṁ bhāvam āśritāḥ* refers to those who are out and out atheists. Although there are no disadvantages to surrendering unto the Father, people who are thus characterized never do it. As a result, they are constantly punished by the agents of the Father. They have to be slapped, caned and kicked severely, and they have to suffer. Just as a father has to chastise his unruly boy, so material nature has to employ certain punishments. At the same time nature is nourishing us by supplying food and other necessities. Both processes are going on because we are sons of the wealthiest Father of all, and Kṛṣṇa is kind even though we do not surrender unto Him. Yet despite being furnished so well by the Father, the *duṣkṛtī* still performs unsanctioned actions. One is foolish if he persists in being punished, and one is low on the human scale if he does not use this human form of life to understand Kṛṣṇa. If a man does not use his life to reawaken the relationship he has with his real Father, he is to be considered fallen in the human scale.

Animals simply eat, sleep, defend themselves, have sexual intercourse and die. They do not avail themselves of higher consciousness because that is not possible in the lower forms of life. If a human being follows the activities of the animals and does not avail himself of his ability to elevate his consciousness, he falls down the human scale and prepares for an animal body in his next life. By the grace of Kṛṣṇa we are given a highly developed body and intelligence, but if we do not utilize them, why should He give them to us again? We must understand that this human body has developed after millions and millions of years of evolution and that in itself it is a chance to get out of the cycle of birth and death in which over eight millions species of life evolve. This chance is given by the grace of Kṛṣṇa, and if we do not take it, are we not the lowest among men? One may be a degree holder–M.A., Ph.D., etc.–from some university, but the illusory energy takes away this mundane knowledge. He who is really intelligent will apply his intelligence to understand who he is, who God is, what material nature is, why he is suffering in material nature, and what is the remedy to this suffering.

We may apply our intelligence to manufacture an automobile, radio or television for sense gratification, but we have to understand that this is not knowledge. Rather, this is plundered intelligence. Intelligence was given to man to understand the problems of life, but it is being misused. People are thinking that they have acquired knowledge because they know how to manufacture and drive cars, but before the car was here people were still going from one place to another. It is just that the facility has been increased, but along with this facility come additional problems—air pollution and over-crowded highways. This is *māyā;* we are creating facilities, but these facilities in their turn are creating so many problems.

Instead of wasting our energy to supply ourselves with so many facilities and modern amenities, we should apply intelligence to understand who and what we are. We do not like to suffer, but we should understand why suffering is being forced upon us. By so-called knowledge we have simply succeeded in manufacturing the atomic bomb. Thus the killing process has been accelerated. We are so proud to think that this is advancement of knowledge, but if we can manufacture something that can stop death, we have really advanced in knowledge. Death is already there in material nature, but we are so eager to promote it by killing everyone at one drop—this is called *māyayāpahṛta-jñāna,* knowledge carried away by illusion.

The *āsuras,* the demons and proclaimed atheists, actually challenge God. If it were not for our Supreme Father, we would not see the light of day, so what is the point of challenging Him? In the *Vedas* it is stated that there are two classes of men, the *devas* and *āsuras,* the demigods and demons. Who are the *devas?* The devotees of the Supreme Lord are called *devas* because they also become like God, whereas those who defy the authority of the Supreme are called *āsuras* or demons. These two classes are always found in human society.

Just as there are four types of miscreants who never surrender to Kṛṣṇa, there are four types of fortunate men who worship Him, and they are categorized in the next verse:

catur-vidhā bhajante māṁ
janāḥ sukṛtino 'rjuna
ārto jijñāsur arthārthī
jñānī ca bharatarṣabha

"O best among the Bhāratas [Arjuna], four kinds of pious men render devotional service unto Me—the distressed, the desirer of wealth, the inquisitive, and he who is searching for knowledge of the Absolute." (Bg. 7.16)

This material world is full of distress, and both the pious and impious are subject to it. The cold of winter treats everyone alike. It does not care for the pious or impious, the rich or the poor. The difference between the pious and the impious, however, is that the pious man thinks of God when he is in his miserable condition. Often when a man is distressed, he will go to church and pray, "Oh my Lord, I am in difficulty. Please help me." Although he is praying for some material necessity, such a man is still to be considered pious because he has come to God in his distress. Similarly, a poor man may go to church and pray, "My dear Lord, please give me some money." On the other hand, the inquisitive are usually intelligent. They are always researching to understand things. They may ask, "What is God?" and then conduct scientific research to find out. They are also considered pious because their research is directed to the proper object. The man in knowledge is called *jñānī*—one who has understood his constitutional position. Such a *jñānī* may have an impersonal conception of God, but because he is taking shelter of the ultimate, the Supreme Absolute Truth, he is also to be considered pious. These four types of men are called *sukṛtī*—pious—because they are all after God.

teṣāṁ jñānī nitya-yukta
eka-bhaktir viśiṣyate
priyo hi jñānino 'tyartham
ahaṁ sa ca mama priyaḥ

"Of these, the wise one who is in full knowledge in union with Me through pure devotional service is the best. For I am very dear to him, and he is dear to Me." (Bg. 7.17)

Out of the four classes of men who approach God, he who is philosophically trying to understand the nature of God, who is trying to become Kṛṣṇa conscious—*viśiṣyate*—is best qualified. Indeed, Kṛṣṇa says that such a person is very dear to Him because he has no other business than understanding God. The others are inferior. No one has to pray to God to ask for anything, and he who does so is foolish because he does not know that the all-knowing God is within his heart and is well aware when he is in distress or in need of money. The wise man realizes this and does not pray for relief from material miseries. Rather, he prays to glorify God and inform others how great He is. He doesn't pray for his personal interest, for bread, dress or shelter. The pure devotee, when he is distressed, says, "Dear Lord, this is Your kindness. You have put me into distress just to rectify me. I should be put in much greater distress, but out of Your mercy You have minimized this." This is the vision of a pure devotee who is not disturbed.

He who is in Kṛṣṇa consciousness does not care for material distress, insult or honor because he is aloof from all these. He knows well that distress, honor and insult pertain to the body only and that he is not the body. Socrates, for instance, who believed in the immortality of the soul, was condemned to death, and upon being asked how he would like to be buried, replied, "First of all you may have to catch me." So one who knows that he is not the body is not disturbed, for he knows the soul cannot be caught, tortured, killed or buried. He who is conversant with the science of Kṛṣṇa knows perfectly well that he is not the body, that he is part and parcel of Kṛṣṇa, that his real relationship is with Kṛṣṇa, and that somehow or other, although he has been put in the material body, he must remain aloof from the three qualities of material nature. He is not concerned with the modes of goodness, passion or ignorance, but with Kṛṣṇa. One who understands this is a *jñānī,* a wise man, and he is very much dear to Kṛṣṇa. A distressed man, when he is put into opulence, may forget God, but a *jñānī,* who knows the real position of God, will never forget Him.

There is a class of *jñānīs* called impersonalists who say that because worshiping the impersonal is too difficult, a form of God has to be imagined. These are not real *jñānīs*—they're fools. No one can imagine the form of God, for God is so great. One may imagine some form, but that is a concoction; it is not the real form. There are those who imagine the form of God, and there are those who deny the form of God. Neither is a *jñānī.* Those who imagine the form are called iconoclasts. During the Hindu-Muslim riots in India, some Hindus would go to the Moslem mosque and would break statues and images of God, and the Moslems would reciprocate in like manner. In this way they were both thinking, "We've killed the Hindu God. We've killed the Moslem God, etc." Similarly, when Gandhi was leading his resistance movement, many Indians would go to the street and destroy the mailboxes and in this way think that they were destroying the government postal service. People of such mentality are not *jñānīs.* The religious wars between the Hindus and Moslems and Christians and non-Christians were all conducted on the basis of ignorance. One who is in knowledge knows that God is one; He cannot be Moslem, Hindu or Christian.

It is our imagination that God is such and such and such and such. That is all imagination. The real wise man knows that God is transcendental. One who knows that God is transcendental to the material modes truly knows God. God is always beside us, present in our hearts. When we leave the body, God also goes with us, and when we take on another body, He goes with us there just to see what we are doing. When shall we turn our face towards Him? He is always waiting. As soon as we turn our face toward God, He says, "My dear son, come on—*sa ca mama priyaḥ*—you are eternally dear to Me. Now you are turning your face to Me, and I am very glad."

The wise man, the *jñānī*, actually understands the science of God. One who only understands that "God is good" is in a preliminary stage, but one who actually understands how great and good God is, is further progressed. That knowledge is to be had in *Śrīmad-Bhāgavatam* and *Bhagavad-gītā*. One who is actually interested in God should study the science of God, *Bhagavad-gītā*.

idaṁ tu te guhyatamaṁ
pravakṣyāmy anasūyave
jñānaṁ vijñāna-sahitaṁ
yaj jñātvā mokṣyase 'śubhāt

"My dear Arjuna, because you are never envious of Me, I shall impart to you this most secret wisdom, knowing which you shall be relieved of the miseries of material existence." (Bg. 9.1)

The knowledge of God imparted in *Bhagavad-gītā* is very subtle and confidential. It is full of *jñāna*, metaphysical wisdom, and *vijñāna*, scientific knowledge. And it is full of mystery also. How can one understand this knowledge? It must be imparted by God Himself or a bona fide representative of God. Therefore Śrī Kṛṣṇa says that whenever there is a discrepancy on understanding the science of God, He incarnates Himself.

Nor does knowledge come from sentiment. Devotion is not sentiment. It is a science. Śrīla Rūpa Gosvāmī says, "A show of spirituality without reference to the Vedic knowledge is simply a disturbance to society." One must taste the nectar of devotion by reason, argument and knowledge, and then he must pass it on to others. One should not think that Kṛṣṇa consciousness is mere sentimentality. The dancing and singing are all scientific. There is science, and there is also loving reciprocation. Kṛṣṇa is very dear to the wise man, and the wise man is very dear to Kṛṣṇa. Kṛṣṇa will return our love a thousand-fold. What capacity do we finite creatures have to love Kṛṣṇa? But Kṛṣṇa has immense capacity —unlimited capacity—for love.

5

Steering Toward the Supreme

udārāḥ sarva evaite
jñānī tv ātmaiva me matam
āsthitaḥ sa hi yuktātmā
mām evānuttamāṁ gatim

"All these devotees are undoubtedly magnanimous souls, but he who is situated in knowledge of Me I consider verily to dwell in Me. Being engaged in My transcendental service, he attains Me." (Bg. 7.18)

Here Kṛṣṇa is saying that all the men who come to Him—whether they be distressed, in need of money, curious, etc.—are welcomed, but out of them the person who is in knowledge is very dear to Him. The others are welcomed because it is understood that in course of time, if they continue on the path to God, they will become as good as the man of knowledge. Generally, however, it so happens that when one goes to church for profit, and the money doesn't come, he concludes that approaching God is nonsense, and he gives up all connection with church. That is the danger of approaching God with ulterior motives. For instance, during World War II it was reported that many wives of the German soldiers went to church to pray for their husbands' safe return, but when they found they had been killed in battle, they became atheistic. Thus we want God to become our order-supplier, and when He does not supply our order, we say that there is no God. That is the effect of praying for material things.

In this connection there is a story of a little boy, about five years old, named Dhruva, who belonged to a royal family. In the course of time his father, the king, tired of his mother and deposed her as his queen. He then took another woman as queen, and she became stepmother to the boy. She was very envious of him, and one day, as Dhruva was sitting on the father's knee, she insulted him. "Oh you cannot sit on the lap of your father," she said, "because you are not born of me." She dragged Dhruva from his father's lap and the boy became very angry. He was the son of a *kṣatriya,* and *kṣatriyas* are notorious for their quick tempers. Dhruva took this to be a great insult, and he went to his mother who had been deposed.

"Dear Mother," he said, "my stepmother has insulted me by dragging me from my father's lap."

"Dear son," the mother replied, "what can I do? I am helpless, and your father no longer cares for me."

"Well, how can I take revenge?" the boy asked.

"My dear boy, you are helpless. Only if God helps you can you take revenge."

"Oh, where is God?" Dhruva asked enthusiastically.

"I understand so many sages go to the jungle and forest to see God," the mother replied. "They undergo great penances and austerities in order to find God there."

At once Dhruva went to the forest and began asking the tiger and the elephant, "Oh, are you God?

Are you God?" In this way he was questioning all the animals. Seeing that Dhruva was very much inquisitive, Śrī Kṛṣṇa sent Nārada Muni to see about the situation. Nārada quickly went to the forest and found Dhruva.

"My dear boy," Nārada said, "you belong to the royal family. You cannot suffer all this penance and austerity. Please return to your home. Your mother and father are very much anxious for you."

"Please don't try to divert me in that way," the boy said. "If you know something about God, or if you know how I can see God, please tell me. Otherwise go away and don't disturb me."

When Nārada saw that Dhruva was so determined, he initiated him as a disciple and gave him the *mantra, om namo bhagavate vāsudevāya.* Dhruva chanted this *mantra* and became perfect, and God came before him.

"My dear Dhruva, what do you want? You can take from Me whatever you want."

"My dear Lord," the boy replied, "I was undergoing such severe penances simply for my father's kingdom and land, but now I have seen You. Even the great sages and saints cannot see You. What is my profit? I left my home to find merely some scraps of glass and rubbish, and instead I have found a very valuable diamond. Now I am satisfied. I have no need to ask anything of You."

Thus even though one may be poverty-stricken or in distress, if he goes to God with the same determination as Dhruva, intent on seeing God and taking His benediction, and if he happens to see God, he will no longer want anything material. He comes to understand the foolishness of material possessions, and he puts the illusion aside for the real thing. When one becomes situated in Kṛṣṇa consciousness, like Dhruva Mahārāja, he becomes fully satisfied and doesn't want anything.

The *jñānī*, the wise man, knows that material things are flickering. He also knows that there are three aspects that complicate all material gain—one wants profit from his work, one wants adoration from others because of his riches, and one wants fame because of his wealth. In any case, he knows that all of these apply but to the body and that when the body is finished, they also go. When the body dies, one is no longer a rich man but a spirit soul, and according to his work, he has to enter another body. The *Gītā* says that a wise man is not bewildered by this, for he knows what is what. Why then should he bother himself attaining material wealth? His attitude is, "I have an eternal connection with Kṛṣṇa, the Supreme Lord. Now let me establish that relationship firmly so that Kṛṣṇa will take me back to His kingdom."

The cosmic situation is giving us all facility to reestablish this relationship with Kṛṣṇa and return to Godhead. This should be our mission in life. Everything we need is being supplied by God—land, grain, fruits, milk, shelter and clothing. We only have to live peacefully and cultivate Kṛṣṇa consciousness. That should be our mission in life. We should therefore be satisfied with what God has supplied in the form of food, shelter, defense and sex, and should not want more and more and more. The best type of civilization is one that ascribes to the maxim of "plain living and high thinking." It is not possible to manufacture food or sex in a factory. These and whatever else we require are supplied by God. Our business is to take advantage of these things and become God conscious.

Although God has given us all facilities to live peacefully on this earth, cultivate Kṛṣṇa consciousness, and finally to come to Him, in this age we're unfortunate. We are short-lived, and there are so many people without food, shelter, married life or defense from the onslaughts of nature. This is due to the influence of this age of Kali. Therefore Lord Caitanya Mahāprabhu, seeing the dreadful situation in this age, emphasized the absolute necessity for cultivating spiritual life. And how should we do it? Caitanya Mahāprabhu gives the formula:

harer nāma harer nāma harer nāmaiva kevalam
kalau nāsty eva nāsty eva nāsty eva gatir anyathā

"Just always chant Hare Kṛṣṇa." Never mind whether you are in a factory or in a hell, in a shack or in a skyscraper–it doesn't matter. Just go on chanting Hare Kṛṣṇa, Hare Kṛṣṇa, Kṛṣṇa Kṛṣṇa, Hare Hare/ Hare Rāma, Hare Rāma, Rāma Rāma, Hare Hare. There is no expense, there is no impediment, there is no caste, there is no creed, there is no color–anyone can do it. Just chant and hear.

Somehow or other, if one comes into contact with Kṛṣṇa consciousness and executes the process under the guidance of a bona fide guide, he is sure to go back to God.

bahūnāṁ janmanām ante
jñānavān māṁ prapadyate
vāsudevaḥ sarvam iti
sa mahātmā sudurlabhaḥ

"After many births and deaths, he who is actually in knowledge surrenders unto Me, knowing Me to be the cause of all causes and all that is. Such a great soul is very rare." (Bg. 7.19)

Philosophical research into the science of God has to be prosecuted for many births. God realization is very easy, but at the same time it is very difficult. It is easy for those who accept Kṛṣṇa's word as truth, but those who try to understand through research work, by dint of advancement of knowledge, have to create their faith after finishing so much research work, and this process takes many births. There are different types of transcendentalists, called *tattvavit,* who know the Absolute Truth. The transcendentalists call the Absolute Truth that in which there is no duality. In the Absolute Truth there is no duality—everything is on the same level. One who knows this in truth is called *tattvavit.*

Kṛṣṇa proclaims that the Absolute Truth is known in three aspects—*Brahman, Paramātmā* and *Bhagavān* —impersonal *Brahman* effulgence, localized Supersoul, and the Supreme Personality of Godhead. Thus there are three angles from which one may envision the Absolute Truth. One may view a mountain from a great distance and thus perceive it from one angle of vision. As he comes closer, he may see the trees and foliage of the mountain, and if he begins to climb the mountain, he will find so much variegatedness in trees, plants and animals. The objective is the same, but due to different angles of vision, sages have different conceptions of the Absolute Truth. Another example: there is the sunshine, the sun disc and the sun god. One who is in the sunshine cannot claim that he is on the sun itself, and one who is situated in the sun is, from the point of view of vision, better situated. The sunshine may be compared to the all-pervasive *brahmajyoti* effulgence, the localized sun-disc may be compared to the localized aspect of the Supersoul, and the sun god who resides within the sun may be compared to the Personality of Godhead. As on this earth planet we have a multivariety of living entities, we can understand from Vedic literatures that in the sun also there is a variety of living entities, but their bodies are made of fire, just as ours are made of earth.

In material nature there are five gross elements: earth, water, air, fire and space. In different planets there are different atmospheres due to one of these five elements prevailing, and there are different bodies for the living entities composed of whatever element may be predominant in a particular planet. We should not think that all planets have the same quality of life, yet there is uniformity in the sense that these five elements are present in some form or other. Thus on some planets earth is prominent, fire is prominent, water is prominent, and air and space are prominent. We should not think, therefore, that just because a planet is not composed primarily of earth, or because the atmosphere does not duplicate ours, that there is no life on these planets. Vedic literatures give us information that there are countless planets filled with living entities with different types of bodies. As, by making some material adjustment, we may qualify to enter into different material planets, by qualification we can enter into the spiritual planet where the Supreme Lord resides.

yānti deva-vratā devān
pitṝn yānti pitṛ-vratāḥ
bhūtāni yānti bhūtejyā
yānti mad-yājino 'pi mām

"Those who worship the demigods will take birth among the demigods; those who worship ancestors go to the ancestors; and those who worship Me will live with Me." (Bg. 9.25)

Those who are trying to enter higher planets can go there, and those who are trying to qualify to enter into Goloka Vṛndāvana, the planet of Kṛṣṇa, can also enter there by the process of Kṛṣṇa consciousness. Before going to India, we may acquire a description of what the country is like; the hearing of a place is the first experience. Similarly, if we want to get information about the planet where God lives, we have to hear. We cannot immediately make an experiment and go there. That is not possible. But we have so many descriptions of the supreme planet in Vedic literature. For instance, the *Brahma-saṁhitā* states:

cintāmaṇi-prakara-sadmasu kalpa-vṛkṣa-
lakṣāvṛteṣu surabhīr abhipālayantam
lakṣmī-sahasra-śata-sambhrama-sevyamānaṁ
govindam ādi-puruṣaṁ tam ahaṁ bhajāmi

"I worship Govinda, the primeval Lord, the first progenitor, who is tending the cows, fulfilling all desire, in abodes built with spiritual gems, surrounded by millions of wish-fulfilling trees, always served with great reverence and affection by hundreds of thousands of *lakṣmīs,* or *gopīs.*" There are also other detailed descriptions given, specifically in *Brahma-saṁhitā.*

Those who are trying to realize the Absolute Truth are categorized according to the aspect of the Absolute Truth upon which they concentrate. Those who concentrate on Brahman, the impersonalists, are called *brahmavādīs.* Generally, those who are trying to realize the Absolute Truth first of all realize the *brahmajyoti.* Those who concentrate on the Supersoul, the localized form of the Lord in the heart, called Paramātmā, are known as *paramātmāvādīs.* The Supreme Lord, by His plenary portion, is sitting in everyone's heart, and by meditation and concentration one can perceive this form. Not only is He within everyone's heart, but He is situated also within every atom of the creation. This Paramātmā realization is the second stage. The third and last stage is the realization of Bhagavān, the Supreme Personality of Godhead. Because there are three main stages of realization, the Supreme Absolute Truth is not attained in one birth. *Bahūnāṁ janmanām ante.* If one is fortunate, he can achieve the ultimate in one second. But generally it takes many, many years and many, many births to realize what God is.

ahaṁ sarvasya prabhavo
mattaḥ sarvaṁ pravartate
iti matvā bhajante māṁ
budhā bhāva-samanvitāḥ

"I am the source of all spiritual and material worlds. Everything emanates from Me. The wise who know this perfectly engage in My devotional service and worship Me with all their hearts." (Bg. 10.8)

The *Vedānta-sūtra* also confirms that the Absolute Truth is He from whom everything is born. If we truly believe that Kṛṣṇa is the origin of everything, and if we worship Him, our whole account is closed in one second. But if one doesn't believe and says, "Oh, I want to see what God is," he has to go by stages by realizing the impersonal Brahman effulgence and then Paramātmā, the localized feature, before finally coming to the last stage of realizing, "Oh, here is the Supreme Personality of Godhead." It should be understood, however, that this process takes more time. When one through many years of research comes to realize the Absolute Truth, he concludes *vāsudevaḥ sarvam iti*—"Vāsudeva is all that is." Vāsudeva is a name for Kṛṣṇa, and it means "He who lives everywhere." Realizing that Vāsudeva is the root of everything—*māṁ prapadyate*—he surrenders. The surrendering process is the ultimate goal; either one does it immediately or after many births of research work. In either case, surrender must be there by realizing that "God is great, and I am His subordinate."

Understanding this, the wise man will surrender immediately and not wait to take many, many births. He understands that this information is given by the Supreme Lord out of His infinite mercy on the conditioned souls. We are all conditioned souls, suffering the threefold miseries of this material world. Now the Supreme Lord is giving us the opportunity to escape these miseries by the surrendering process.

At this point one may ask that if the Supreme Personality is the ultimate goal and one has to surrender to Him, why are there so many different processes of worship in the world? This question is answered in the next verse.

kāmais tais tair hṛta-jñānāḥ
prapadyante 'nya-devatāḥ
taṁ taṁ niyamam āsthāya
prakṛtyā niyatāḥ svayā

"Those whose minds are distorted by material desires surrender unto demigods and follow the particular rules and regulations of worship according to their own natures." (Bg. 7.20)

There are many different types of men in the world, and they're functioning under the different modes of material nature. Generally speaking, most men are not after liberation. If they take to spirituality, they wish to gain something by spiritual power. It is not uncommon in India for a person to go to a *svāmī* and say, "Svāmījī, could you give me some medicine? I am suffering from this disease." He thinks that because a doctor is too expensive, he can go to a *svāmī* who can work miracles. In India also there are *svāmīs* who go to people's houses and preach, "If you give me one ounce of gold I can make it into one hundred ounces of gold." The people think, "I have five ounces of gold. Let me give it to him, and I'll get five hundred ounces." In this way the *svāmī* collects all the gold in the village, and after collecting it, he vanishes. This is our disease: when we go to a *svāmī,* or a temple or a church, our hearts are filled with material desires. Wanting some material profit out of spiritual life, we practice *yoga* just to keep our health fit. But, in order to keep healthy, why take shelter of *yoga?* We can become healthy through regular exercises and regulated diet. Why resort to *yoga?* Because: *kāmais tais tair hṛta-jñānāḥ.* We have the material desire to keep ourselves fit and to enjoy life by going to church and making God our order-supplier.

Having material desires, men worship various demigods. They have no idea how to get out of matter; they want to utilize the material world to its best capacity. For instance, in Vedic literature there are so many recommendations: if one wants to cure his disease, he worships the sun, or if a girl wants a good husband, she worships Lord Śiva, or if one wants to become beautiful, he worships such and such god, or if one wants to become educated, he worships goddess Sarasvatī. In this way Westerners often think that the Hindus are polytheistic, but actually this worship is not to God, but to demigods. We should not think that the demigods are God. God is one, but there are demigods who are also living entities just like us. The difference is that they have a considerable amount of power. On this earth there may be a king or a president or a dictator—these are men like us, but they have some extraordinary power, and in order to get favors from them, to take advantage of their power, we worship them in one way or another. But *Bhagavad-gītā* condemns worship of the demigods. This verse clearly states that people worship the demigods due to *kāma,* material lust.

This material life is simply based on lust; we want to enjoy this world, and we love this material world because we want to gratify our senses. This lust is a perverted reflection of our love of God. In our original constitution we are made to love God, but because we have forgotten God, we love matter. Love is there. Either we love matter, or we love God. But in no case can we get out of this loving propensity; indeed, we often see that when one doesn't have children, he loves a cat or a dog. Why? Because we want and need to love something. In the absence of reality, we put our faith and love in cats and dogs. Love is always there, but it is distorted into the form of lust. When this lust is baffled, we become angry; when we become angry, we become illusioned; and when we are illusioned, we are doomed. This is the process that is going on, but we have to reverse this process and turn lust into love. If we love God, we love everything. But if we do not love God, it is not possible to love anything. We may think that it is love, but it is simply a glamorized form of lust. Those who have become the dogs of lust are said to have lost all good sense: *kāmais tais tair hṛtajñānāḥ.*

There are many rules and regulations for the worship of demigods in the scriptures, and one may question why the Vedic literatures recommended their worship. There is necessity. Those who are motivated by lust want the opportunity to love something, and the demigods are acknowledged as the officers of the Supreme Lord. The idea is that as one worships these demigods, he will gradually develop Kṛṣṇa consciousness. But if one is completely atheistic and disobedient and rebellious against any authority, what hope is there? So one's obedience to a higher personality can start with the demigods.

If, however, we take directly to the worship of the Supreme Lord, worship of the demigods is not necessary. Those who worship the Supreme Lord directly show all respect to the demigods, but they do not need to worship them because they know that the supreme authority behind the demigods is the Supreme Personality of Godhead, and they are engaged in worshiping Him. In any case, respect is still there. A devotee of the Lord shows respect even to an ant, what to speak of the demigods? The devotee is aware that all living entities are parts and parcels of the Supreme Lord and that they are playing different roles only.

In relation to the Supreme Lord, all beings are to be respected. Therefore a devotee refers to others as "Prabhu," meaning "My dear sir, my dear lord." Submissiveness is a qualification for a devotee of the Lord. Devotees are kind and obedient, and they have all good qualifications. In conclusion, if one becomes a devotee of the Lord, all good qualifications will automatically develop. By nature, the living entity is perfect, but due to the contamination of lust, he becomes vicious. That which is part and parcel of gold is also gold, and whatever is part and parcel of the Complete Perfect is also perfect.

om pūrṇam adaḥ pūrṇam idaṁ
pūrṇāt pūrṇam udacyate
pūrṇasya pūrṇam ādāya
pūrṇam evāvaśiṣyate

"The Personality of Godhead is perfect and complete. Because He is completely perfect, all emanations from Him, such as this phenomenal world, are perfectly equipped as a complete whole. Whatever is produced of the complete whole is also complete in itself. Because He is the complete whole, even though so many complete units emanate from Him, He remains the complete balance." (*Śrī Īśopaniṣad*, Invocation)

Due to the contamination of matter, the perfect living entity falls down, but this process of Kṛṣṇa consciousness will again make him perfect. Through it, he can become truly happy, and after leaving the material body, enter into the kingdom where there is eternal life, bliss and full knowledge.

ISKCON CENTERS AROUND THE WORLD

ISKCON is a worldwide community of devotees dedicated to the principles of *bhakti-yoga*. Write, call, or visit for further information. Classes are held in the evenings during the week, and a special feast and festival is held every Sunday afternoon.

AFRICA: **Nairobi, Kenya**—c/o ISKCON, P.O. Box 28946 (E. Africa)

THE AMERICAS: **Atlanta, Georgia**—24 NE 13th Street/ (404)892-9042; **Austin, Texas**—9714 Dallum/ (512)837-0085; **Bloomington, Indiana**—1130 W. 6th St./ (812)336-5306; **Boston, Massachusetts**—40 N. Beacon Street/ (617)782-8892; **Buffalo, New York**—132 Bidwell Pkwy./ (716)882-0281; **Chicago, Illinois**—1014 Emerson St., Evanston/ (312)864-1343; **E. Cleveland, Ohio**—15720 Euclid Avenue/ (216)451-0418; **Dallas, Texas**—5430 Gurley St./ (214)827-6330; **Denver, Colorado**—1400 Cherry Street/ (303)322-6661; **Detroit, Michigan**—8311 E. Jefferson Avenue/ (313)824-6000; **Honolulu, Hawaii**—2016 McKinley Street/ (808)949-9022; **Houston, Texas**—707 Hawthorne; **Laguna Beach, California**—641 Ramona Avenue/ (714)494-9172; **Los Angeles, California**—3764 Watseka Avenue/ (213)871-0717; **Mexico City, Mexico**—Gobernador Tiburcio Montiel No. 45, San Miguel/ (905)515-4242; **Miami, Florida**—363 N.W. 4th St./ (305)377-2191; **Montreal, Quebec**—3720 Park Avenue, Canada/ (514)849-4319; **New Orleans, Louisiana**—2936 S. Esplanade/ (504)482-6406; **New Vṛndāvana, W. Virginia**—RD 3, Moundsville/ (304)845-2790; **New York, New York**—439 Henry Street, Brooklyn/ (212)596-9658; **Philadelphia, Pennsylvania**—641 E. Chelten Ave./ (215)849-1767; **Pittsburgh, Pennsylvania**—5135 Ellsworth Avenue/ (412)683-7700; **Portland, Oregon**—2507 NE Stanton Street/ (503)284-6395; **St. Louis, Missouri**—4544 Laclede Avenue/ (314)361-1224; **San Diego, California**—3300 3rd Avenue/ (714)291-7778; **San Francisco, California**—455 Valencia St./ (415)864-9233; **Seattle, Washington**—400 18th Avenue East/ (206)329-9348; **Toronto, Ontario**—187 Gerrard St. East, Canada/ (416)922-5415; **Vancouver-9, British Columbia**—1786 West 11th Avenue, Canada/ (604)732-8422; **Washington, D.C.**—2015 "Q" Street NW/ (202)667-3516

ASIA: **Calcutta, India**—3 Albert Road/ 44-3757; **Delhi, India**—Cottage Street No. 9, Gurugreh, West Patel Nagar; **Hare Kṛṣṇa Land, India**—ISKCON, Nairwadi, Gandhi Gram Rd., Juhu, Bombay 54; **Jakarta, Indonesia**—P.O. Box 2640; **Manila, Philippines**—179 Ortega Street, San Juan Rizal; **Mayapur, India**—ISKCON International Center, P.O. Sree Mayapur Dham, W. Bengal (District Nadia); **Tokyo, Japan**—5-12-2, 2 Bancho Chiyoda-ku; **Vṛndāvana, India**—ISKCON, Rādhā-Dāmodara Temple, Seva Kunj, Mathurā, U.P.; **Vṛndāvana, India**—ISKCON, Raman Reti, Mathurā. U.P.

AUSTRALIA: **Adelaide, Australia**—1 Rossington Ave., Myrtlebank, S.A.; **Auckland, New Zealand**—67 Gribblehirst Rd., Mt. Albert/ 668-666; **Brisbane, Australia**—19 Douglas St., Milton, Queensland 4064; **Melbourne, Australia**—14 Burnett St., St. Kilda, Victoria 3182; **Sydney, Australia**—83 Hereford Street, Glebe 2037, N.S.W./ 660-7159

EUROPE: **Amsterdam, Holland**—Bethanienstraat 39 (C) 020-3502607; **Berlin, W. Germany**—1 Berlin-69, Nordbahn Str. 3; **Edinburgh, Scotland**—14 Forest Road; **Geneva, Switzerland**—9, chemin due Credo, 1213 Petit Lancy; **Hamburg, W. Germany**—2 Hamburg 54, Kapitalbushweg 20/ 570-53-82; **Heidelberg, W. Germany**—69 Heidelberg 1, Karlsruherstrasse 31354; **London-WC 1, England**—7 Bury Place/ 01-242-0394; **Lyon, France**—4, rue Sala; **Munich, W. Germany**—8 Munchen 40, Josephsplatz 4/I; **Paris, France**—26 bis, Rue d'Estienne d'Ovres, 92 Fontenay aux Roses